MW01104239

BONES

BONES

Tyler Pennock

Brick Books

Library and Archives Canada Cataloguing in Publication

Title: Bones / Tyler Pennock.
Names: Pennock, Tyler, 1977– author.
Description: Poems.
Identifiers: Canadiana (print) 20190238291 | Canadiana (ebook) 20190238321 | ISBN 9781771315210 (softcover) | ISBN 9781771315227 (HTML) | ISBN 9781771315234 (PDF)
Classification: LCC PS8631.E56 B66 2020 | DDC C811/.6—dc23

We acknowledge the Canada Council for the Arts, the Government of Canada through the Canada Book Fund, and the Ontario Arts Council for their support of our publishing program.

The author photo was taken by Aaron Bowerman.

The book is set in Dante.

Design and layout by Marijke Friesen.
Cover image by Ovila Mailhot.

Printed and bound by Coach House Printing.

Brick Books
115 Haliburton Road
London, ON
N6K 2Z2

www.brickbooks.ca

Kiwaaciyemaanaanak Kimishoomisinaanak

Under the moonlight
the softness that night gives us –
        the earth rising to meet
        in snow, or the glow of trilliums
where there is enough sound in a breath –

in here
I speak

gently step
        and story-weave
sending out a thread of me

like a foot's condensation
drying on a summer floor

hoping the memory of me
        survives
                in the eyes of others

I'll speak
of blood

and wounds and beauty
in terrible things

the way the wind pulls a thousand leaves
        down an empty street

and when they settle –
                we look up
                to trace the direction of the wind

Snow

stretches, grasps
the frigid air
        directions pulled
from a liquid
slowly dying

A starburst of water
        branch of light
crystallized
        amidst darkness
the dance played out
in fractal precision

Elsewhere, uniform shadow
        reveals the same

        liquid and night caressing each other

the touch of careful lovers coupling

in solitude
while falling toward a canopy

of one hundred billion captured lights

        •

The bitter cold
and tender touch

of frozen lights falling
reminds me of the softest
and deepest sleep

the kind that won't wait
takes you on the stairs
            with one shoe on
            laces still on the floor

the kind that rides
waves of awareness
            where the conversations
            mingle easily with approaching dreams

like driving through whiteouts
            in the early morning of your third day without sleep

This, the pleasing, bitter cold
determined and strong

comes easily

leading me
to the soothing and explosive

meeting place of myself
            and my memory

•

I wished I was soft like water

a thought caught me
        entangled – every struggling twitch away from it
                tightened the hold

like a fly trapped in a web,
        tightening, pulling
        eight legs closer
        as gravity
                pulls stars

The thought that grabbed me
                and squeezed all the way to dinner

I wish I was like water – no sharp edges

was a memory as strong as a child's will
burning through my life

old age and entropy
        pulling flesh downward, from bone
        and the memory of us

                Our actions, our intent –
                    lost to rot

•

After my third cigarette,
           and before dinner . . .

shadow sent out a limb –
           its origin, I knew

Underneath haleq
           the deepest wave
           (well below the surface)
           and the reach of any star
           or captured light

     my chest gave way to worry

and I heard the final crack
           of chains, doors
           breaking open

     •

Thanksgiving –

snapshots of this table
lit my senses, brought me out
of my stupor

Cranberry sauce, untouched
                              barely from the can

        teased
        the pallid beauty of the tablecloth
        offering the sweetness of a touch
        and the slow exploration of red on white

              drip

              drip

              drip

              drip

        •

Fear takes any form it can steal
and wears it – like elegance at a gala
            replete with broad smiles

a world of comfort wrapped around you

Fear has a way of building itself
out
of the deepest cells
        scars breeding as a fire might
        on dry grass

It is always something inside
that the world eventually teases out

The most hurtful things
can't impact the space
one's own nightmares hold –

                    (twenty years ago)
            the force of a cue ball in a shoe bag
            at the apogee
            of my boyfriend's hardest throw
            wasn't enough

I was safe
Standing over him,
bleeding
        on his face, I knew:

No act can harm me
the worst has been done

Back then,
terror
had much further to travel
to get past the scar tissue

       but fear
       is inquisitive
       stubborn

•

Tonight, I don't know
what brought me here
I hardly remember
where I am
                        how many street lamps I passed
I am scared –

                                            Something grins

inhaled, hardened, and expelled

Thrown

from my feet –
alarm
grating joints and muscles seizing
like rust on a chain-link fence, left

with the sluggish feeling of panic –
                            all reactions, all options
                                        fleeing
as my face approached the unyielding force of stone

Will my blood congeal
leak my senseless thoughts
be tainted by something else?

Who knows such things?

I remember once he said
I can't control how you receive my words

    •

In the centre
of a small depression

Emergency

two paths cross
In darkness, straining

to illuminate the walkway
an odd blue light
The stuff of ghosts

Its silence a reminder of times past –
when violence lurked in the darkness behind buildings
underneath canopied walkways
you weren't supposed to breach
                                    at night

When terror was assumed
people thought choice meant safety
and Canada wasn't responsible
for its victims

The blue light at the corner of two paths
offers safety police badges, smiling men

I walk now, knowing
            at one time I would not belong

The blue light assures me
            a few metres from where white boys played football
            and engaged in hazing

Blue light
assuring we all now belong
            A few steps beyond a plaque
            among fourteen trees – each for a woman memorialized

    •

The body is a collection
    of continuously dying cells

        destroying
        to repair   .

        memory held
        not through physical means
        but electrical impulses

moving beyond
        flesh
        like the force of dying
        suns crushed
        a black hole's only trace
        being the ghost it sends out
        perpendicular to the stars it killed

If the body is a collection
        of continuously dying cells

then I am memory
        each destruction of me
refolded into me

more than scars bursting
        pain and harm

memory passed to new, stronger cells

A reprint –

    each armed with knowing

    and stronger than the last

•

Lying here

in the intersection of dying cells

and rising memory

I wonder
        which parts of me
        will matter
most –

if my head
opened and spilling
its pieces

makes sense to you
as it does to me

would these moments
        rising

draw the same lines
patterns
through time?

Or
        as reader
        watcher
        consumer
        devourer

does all the meaning rest
with you instead?

(Your power should make you cautious)

•

Our living room seemed infected
        with the waning sunshine that chased us out past curfew
        and an impatient moon, up before the stars –

        things not in their time

The ironing board that never strayed far from the front door
        where the sound of steam escaping steel
        announced our father's presence, or how

        we all knew to press a shirt
        from watching his habits –
        where he placed the creases
        so that they stayed

I used to ask
        him to show me again
        but the repetition
        could never burn into me
        the right way to do it

        •

There were cardboard boxes
      in the basement for moving
      with areas for rank, family name, and unit number

      You used to teach me to read
      words like *story, dog, Shasta,* and *lasagna*
      Sioux, Blackfoot, princess

      The words that I later realized described us
      words our parents used in lieu of any real understanding
      scrambling like we did in the dark

      boxes everywhere
      covered with pen and crayoned words

•

Suitcases –
in the closets, under all the beds
      filling all the free space
      ready to move
      sometimes for years

The repeated injury of lost friends
and lost landmarks
      like the cornfields that ran behind the house
      where we played predator
      or the smoke stack above Dow Chemical
      where we caught the bus for school

were normalized by the constant presence of suitcases
we were used to them
we were used to change

comforted by teal hard cases, floral canvas, every shade of beige
and so much brown

Like calluses, they were the hard skin to protect the injured skin
    underneath

Now I struggle
to find a suitcase when I need it

I've grown soft
in my comfort

    •

There was a kindness to you
      a quiet hush

another secret added
      to the world we cradled together
      a candle in the sandstorm – you

reaching out from the kitchen window
      holding a plate with two pork chops
      soggy broccoli

      the steam rising in sunlight

refracted by the snow
      a single tiny cloud –
                  I never forgot

      how the things you did
      always came in secret

•

Family gatherings

were the best times
        because laughter is contagious

We could return to being children

while we shared food
        You gave me the chicken skin, gristle, bones
        while I gave you the healthier things . . .

It was never the groups of people
        that procured my smiles

        but you –
        the food exchange a re-enactment
        for all the times you rescued me
        our private ceremony

shared memories
        branding me

I've always tried to repay you in kind for your presence
        and could only manage love, and admiration
        for your strength – surviving things I could not

shared beauty
        in a throng of rough
        unfinished souls

        •

Remembering summer
and lying under trees – looking up

how I enjoyed the incomplete
nature of leaves
the way they blended into each other
in the wind, and sunlight

I loved how
       sky and cloud were interrupted, softened

       sunlight turning as it rolled, falling down –
       wild innumerable interruptions

       the sun's inconstant nature
       (blistering and distant cold in span of a year)

       softened somehow

       wishing
       the bruises, isolation
       cuts, the cold and brutal love

       we received in multi-coloured abundance

could be tempered
       by a summer of our own

•

Night clawed at the street lamps pushing back
        at the light, suspicious

        away from houses, cars, roads, clock radios
        and televisions – the manufactured
        comforts of the world
        we were adopted into

We darted between circles
of light on the pavement
        while breathing houses
        amplified our voices
                                We watched

how the light clung to our shadows on the grass
        admiring the halos around our heads

        pretending

        to be angels
        watching

        without fear

        while the
        world slept

        •

There's nothing like a little fog
     to soften things a bit
     at 1:00 a.m.

turning dark angled spaces
     into rounded echoes

Our shadows growing

     taking our laughter with them –

   •

On your birthday I remember
the cake she made

that we didn't expect
        our faces masks of fear

(we never liked the unexpected)

We sat staring at the cake
and her smile, twitching

Her dark moments began to show
        a lot those days

You assured me with a wink
                        something other
                        than me
                        would break

        •

When a child learns
        amid the fear of something
        terrible

        the fragility of their parent

something shatters
        inside them –
        the
dual crush
of fear and empathy

        •

In front of me, the cake bled itself onto the paper
fuchsia, green, and azure dyes invaded the pristine surface
Like a pen stroke interrupted

my thoughts poured out
wild, over the kitchen table

•

I didn't understand the world of that house –
      the walls, books, silver-plated stereo

All I knew was that you were there
      a perfect ghost

invisible to all but me

slipping in like a fog signal
      and offering gifts in exchange for a smile, or perhaps –

> *It'll snow again*
> *but I think you'll be let in*
>
> *soon . . .*
>
> *If you eat this*
> *you won't be cold anymore*
>
> *When you come in*
> *I'll steal hot chocolate*

    – perhaps a little hope.

•

I used to hoard Halloween candy all year
kept it for the times I wasn't allowed to eat

but more for the transgression
denying them the satisfaction of seeing me hungry

(hiding things became my defiance)

I remember once, after filling myself on molasses kisses

Dad invited me down for dinner
    made just for me

I cried, worried
    that I had somehow hurt him

•

When the world went dark
        our parents chiselled at the darkness
        with candles and flashlights

while we hid in our bedrooms
on either side of our shared closet wall

carving away at the drywall
        telling secrets

    peering

        into holes we'd made
        realizing that we'd dug in different spots

        •

For two months I lived by a sliver of light
under the basement door

                              At night

I would curl myself up
on the top three steps

pulling the light over my shoulder
down my back and around my ankles

listening to the voices in the kitchen
pretending to be part of them

mouthing the words like I was there

Listening to you talk was
the connection I stole

happy like a ghost
present, but untouchable

Invisibility became my greatest power

Later, it grew
                    It grew like the shadow cast by our roof
toward Jenny Beland's house at night

As a teenager, I took pleasure from looking into other houses
imagining hidden things, like breakfast before school

my own piece of beautiful
while wandering the winter city at night
because it was safer to sleep outside in the daytime

As the darkness grew
so did my tiny sliver of light

a pleasure I cradled and fostered
and stole whatever light she allowed

•

Looking back
deep inside the spark

that started this –
        I'd wish from the world

that we could put a switch in our parents
so this rage could be carried somewhere

away from us

and the electric train we broke

and the basement door

that held me

far longer than two months

        •

It's funny how a child's comfort can grow
in any place – how the place

of my many punishments
became the heart
of my greatest comfort, I don't know

Was it those two lights I befriended
in the dark that first night, or the fact

my sister
taught me to read down there

a combination of these things, or
if – like many children –
my independence grew early

(before its time)

Now, basements are my soft space
the only space I can sleep soundly

•

There are sharks underneath my bed
you've never seen them

(you have your own)

They circle around me
waiting for a slip

I tie my blankets around the posts
so as not to let the light from the flashlight out

If they know I'm awake
they'll start circling again

I read that sharks are attracted to panic, forget

there's creak coming from the bed
when I lean toward the window, fear

the vibrations creeping out, alerting
the sharks to my presence

I breathe through my mouth, hoping
they will not hear

me squeezing out tears, I imagine
you sleeping as the doorknob turns

letting the sharks in to feast

•

If we put sadness out
sadness will meet us

If we imagine badness
badness will greet us

What we seek we'll catch
spirit's face changed to
match

like the two spirits I met in the basement

and the ones you told me about –
ghosts of the Indian world

something handwritten in a found book

hidden
under the Lazy Susan
wrapped in a towel Mom thought lost

•

After a night of sliding off the garage roof onto piled snow
we sat and looked up at the stars –
        a thousand eyes in night's dress

Something in me then
wanted to live up to your kindness
your praise and attention

I knew I could remember better
if I closed my eyes repeatedly, like camera flashes

a suitable response for a boy who by then made a habit of hiding things
(other signs of love were already exhausted out of me by then)

That was how I would remember that day
        to bring it back to you
        wrapped in brotherly fondness, so that

you could smile at the care I took to remember

        Years later, when I recalled it for us
        you said you didn't remember that

you were too busy remembering all the harm done to me
        my witness

        •

Also

       years later

             they would call my camera flashes

                     a compulsion – brought on by trauma

I still cry at this

    •

I heard that people forget the hardest memories
        the traumas of our lives

like rust –
water and air

destroying the bond between hard things
and the shape of them dissolves

                    aware
                    every time a devourer
                    swallowed a piece of me

leaving depressions in my skin
        that wouldn't come out
        for years

        •

It was such a flimsy chain
barely held together

the knot compromised by Mom's uncertainty – knowing
she'd hurt us, fearing

the consequences, too late
afraid
to show weakness

That was the madness you said
you saw in her eyes

I was pinned to the stairs

your face blurring as you backed up

I'm leaving
                    I'll send help

•

Even in memory
entropy doesn't allow choice

disappearing things
don't get to retain their shape

as my mind sealed off terrible things
my memory of your presence went with them

and I was alone
        to remember you better
I had to remember
all of it

I searched for you between things
Mom did

        but I would never be able
        to cut up the memory of our family
        as well as I wished

You told me once that there are only soft things
in your dreams – and that I could have them

if I wanted

        •

The threads that held us together
       mother and son

being spun of all the things we shared
       appeared tangled then

but weren't
       We overlooked a pattern
       so old and regular
       that it felt automatic to us

the centre of it – the part from which all movement started –

was, for a boy
       the smallest space, yet
       capable of consuming galaxies

was, for her
       the dark space between stars

On one side, she
was desperately pulling – her arms around me
like a mass of hurtled suns
toward dark

On the other
       me
       seeing the darkness
       pushing away

Deep in the middle of our fear
a mother fearing loss
a son fearing mother – fearing harm

Appetite in human form

•

This is why I smoke

...if the body is a collection
      of continuously dying cells

then are we not the same –
         our deaths serving to make the whole stronger?

Is our blood not a constant flow of memories

     shaped

to make us survive what our parents could not?

    •

I learned a new skill that year

It started when I pulled my consciousness
      like a red-stained dress

up past my chest and shoulders
up into the very back of my head

where no sound or touch
could be felt

            and provided my own tenderness

                              I could feel my hands swell
                        slow the sensation leaving them

                                    and for a moment
                                    I was a giant

                        larger than the house I was in

      •

Mrs. Miller told us that water expands when it freezes
stretches out in all directions

filling the space around it
sometimes breaking the container it's in

Later, I learned that water could trap and bend light
the same way we turn feelings into memory

I sat at the desk, head down
squeezing my eyes

trying to blot out all the distractions of that house
to get to my memories of you

holding snapshots of bad memories
that would one day thaw –

or in freezing them
perhaps they would crack
and explode, shatter

the house
in which they formed

•

I started dreaming of another house then, a place without shadows. Every wall was white – every feature etched out. There were no windows, no doors – only white on white.

In this house I knew there was a young girl – the brown of her sending insult to the rooms around us. I could feel her, as though her breath could travel around every corner, and touch even the numbest soul. But I could never see, or find her.

The last time I tried, I could hear the machines outside, trying to erase the house entirely. And I raced through the rooms, testing my voice against the almost featureless walls.

As everything fell around me, I felt her fear – possibly for the last time.

•

My sister –

I wonder if she let the softness in her slip
        like a grip held too long –
        blood and sweat
        lubricate an exit
(force and fear creating the thing we try to prevent) –

and goodness fell away to gravity

I wonder if she left the space of those thoughts the same way
        I did, or if she had another –

a way that grew in the wake of such gentleness – distress

thieving our awareness
        running away with our future
                                I wondered

what her door to escape looked like
        whether it was her leaving her physical body
        or crying on the bathroom floor
        holding a knife

        •

Stockholm syndrome –

the words
stick, roll back
down the inside of my throat, congealing
imprisoning my thoughts

They feed Wiihtikook –
that hunger
for unfinished things
whose currency is fear
and confusion

My breath
pulls
my mind
downward through my stomach, my thighs
through the floor
        and away

I am constricted
My thoughts painted over
A faint shadow behind

•

                        Help me
My words
are not my own – imprisoned
crippled by two tongues
                                    How   can
        I
                un-knit
                                                        the
                            of
                    order
                                            Middle

Beginning
                                                            End?
                        and

Not today, Jesus –

                    not today

I'd like to meet the boy who dreamed me

　　　out of the example
　　　left by his father –
　　　or mother?

Or perhaps the parents

he's seen in other families
　　　shadows
　　　cast by the outline of strangers
　　　　　　　　　　　　　Ask him

what created the shape of me
　　　that he thought he'd step into

If he'd met me then
　　　would he have agreed
　　　to continue? Or was the shape he created

just shy of the mold, and
if so

what helped him
fill in the gaps?

　　•

Take me now –
      smash me on the ground
      create littered shards
      of broken glass
      and make a single image
      out of many, build

a story that isn't mine
      Make it born of fire and wind, cold winters
      a *new* world given
      to broken things

Make something whole again

Go ahead

it's okay
      don't worry about the damage you'll create –

      we've survived it before

    •

I'm adopted, yes
Grown, indeed

But the feeding didn't end there

(it rarely does)

As my birth mother
resists men's offers along highway 2
someone recounts the time he was held down by his cousin
my friend describes leaving the continent to escape her man
and her journey to recover her children from him later
my uncles relive the shame of their oldest brother's
brokerage
of younger siblings

while my grandmother struggled to lift her head

My blood relatives refuse to have children
fearing they will do the same –

while I cannot hold my nephews
because of the shame
I am afraid I will repeat

I recount this all –

going down on a man whose belly hides his face
and I am thankful

while his eczema spots
stare at me, laughing

my shame good enough for a paying stranger
but not for his disease

This, I am used to
The consequence of devouring –
contagious

•

Puking

>   in his bathroom
>   I realized –

>   >   we were made trading love for hunger

•

Out of survival
        I became food
        in a world where no one is sated

peddler of my own flesh, and anything
        they needed

still surprised
        at the ones who needed
                feeling

a night of company
        an added layer
        over exposed muscle

a protection so thin
        it needed constant remaking

•

The way that light cut into me

not just then, but often
                              – over the decades it would return

like the shape of your foot
on the inside of your favorite shoes

A presence made warm, comfortable
        and regular over time

                Until your shoes wear
                and you put on new ones
                But slowly, the imprint returns

The light of that house returned in the same way
                building comfort inside things

                Terrifying to a child

to a man

As child, I always knew we lived
                in a world of fences, borders, and trapped things

                made comfortable
                by repetition
                borders as natural as imaginary

so comfortable
we thought we made them

        •

I had a friend who would press his hand on the accumulating ice in a
    freezer
repeatedly, over months
until his hand claimed its own space
in the deep freeze

In my habit I imagined the imprint
of a hardened hand on the soul

of a child
                turned adult
turned child again

by memories that won't give up
their hold
ice giving way
to repetition and the slow melt
the slow and lustful
        surrender of one force to another

the learned helplessness of the ice matching the despair

of a child
        turned adult
turned child again

fractal beauty melted
by frequent – unprepared – unsafe, touch

In the light-memory held by the ice
        we are dissembled

        •

What is it about shadow that clings
to us so well?

How are we compelled

to stare into darkness
        step into its fold
        swim beneath the waves
        of every little thing it promises

to unknit

        disintegrate

                and pull us under?

How does the lust for injury
        and the appeal for destruction
                sit in the deeper parts of us? I ask

because I'd like to meet with it
        sit with it
        understand
        its curiosity

        how it stalks like a twink
        around the edges of
        a dance floor

desire leaking out
like infection

eye contact an invitation
      to sacred things
      where the light is recalcitrant
      scared to enter

where mutual destruction
sweat, and regret collaborate
      for a moment

covering

the deeper things we need

•

I am sacred!

he screamed into the sky
Stopping to grin in self-satisfaction before the bottle hit the passing train

he wobbled on one foot
the open air dancing around and under his converse one-stars
that somehow gripped the steel like spiders

Wishing I could dance around convention
the way he danced around safety

I chose to hide the tightness of my cheeks around this foolish grin
and the forming tightness in my pants

He knew anyway
and he loved that I appreciated
how sacred he was

•

I wonder if my attraction to men
       is preceded by my understanding
       of their capacity for violence?

Or if the opposite is more likely?

Is my attraction
       to you
       dominated
       by my fear of the other side –
       the chaos it brought
       to the edges of our house
       and our imaginings?

(Sharp corners

       making us bleed)

   •

Unprepared – I fell

for him

telling him I liked the madness of wind
      and bright water
                         He
looking at me like I was mad
      but smiling in a way only the closest friends can

I wondered if such things
could last

    •

If I was just a shoulder, could I touch you with the rounded part?

Could I slide my entire being down your back and ask you to notice?

Or turn myself around and float away
      so that even this small part of me is unknown to you?

Should I wait until you touch me?

Will small bumps mar my skin?

Will shivers outline the small of my back?

Will tremors sculpt the length of my thighs?

Will the air sear my inner places
      as my chest fills with remembering

– the body I once had?

•

Time

is slipping down the wall
gripping imperfection –

tears at the paint

pulls our eyes to the floor
where the weight of
lost expectations
settles, turns

where your elbow meets the wall
writhes in the folds of your clothing, switching
back and forth
pulling at your sleeves
confusing me –

finally weary
you rest your hands in your pockets
shuffle your feet
and look away

Jumping between us
it thieves our words

senses victory
splashes on the floor
and disappears –

seeing it leave I look up
as you tell me you don't have time

I nod and turn to the door

Above our heads
another moment forms

                              – anxious to steal

    •

Time never stops stealing
     we race toward each other

while the worst of it pulls us back
     and we die quickly

like the largest stars
     their strength forcing a quick demise

     a ride too short to be remembered

Time never stops
     I think to myself
     waiting again
     for his return

with a pack of frozen peas on my temple

The shame of us –
     the way a star's brute light
     ensures a quick return to blackness

•

Could there be a way to measure
what is done in anger
scoring the hatred and selfishness
piled in neatly arranged numbers

What is done in anger
tears at you like rain
3324 frozen needles every hour
un-noticeable, stealing with each touch

tears at you like rain
ripping feeling from your skin
un-noticeable, stealing with each touch
in almost rational patterns

ripping feeling from your skin
in ways you cannot trace
completely irrational patterns
the scars left in feeling's place

•

I don't think people understand
        that needles and knives

are gifts
to be reused

Sending different painful things
        away from us, into others

rather than lose the warmth
        of connection
        we turn and force others to bleed it for us

                I wonder if I should thank
                those ikowinak kakiipiniikaaniwaac and the ways

                they built this into my body

                perhaps –

                are there other reasons to point to?
                Other people to thank?

No one is left
        to blame

        •

These must be the thoughts that led me

to wake beside a blue lamp
in the middle of a university campus

Emergency

Some thought of safety
That pulled me here

some promise of protection from
the memory of all this

something in the offer of protection
from white men

. . .

made by other white men

No –

I won't find safety here

safety doesn't come in blue

•

I used to dream of sunlight behind drawn blinds
      – a terrible, vengeful sunlight

smashing through the windows at terrifying speed
      the awful yellow of those walls

My sister told me there were only sharp things in her dreams now
      I said she could have mine, if she wanted

She said no, she kind of liked her dreams
      of sunlight behind stained glass

brilliant colours cut into hard shapes

I wish I could remember you in soft ways
but those memories only come sharp

    •

I remember the laboured breathing coming from the basement – the slanted light that entered the house mimicking the breaths, until the house itself was moving. In there, the shadows were my solace, the light a threat.

I dreamt that I was being pulled into the basement, where the breathing pounded out all my memory. I remember the screams I knew were down there, that never made it beyond the door.

In a house where comfort was cannibal –

like prey, lying down and giving in to their pursuer

my safety was my ending

•

Outward my thoughts flow
    searching for promontories

ululating
    a slow wave stretching away from me

Outcroppings inch themselves closer
    eager to taste

and a moment of understanding sparks from our touch –
    a world born

Am I now found?

    •

If you feel something
if you fear something

if something grows
    of past wrongs
    and deep scars
    and the foolish choices
    of young parents
    or the insatiable desire
    of old men

name it

•

Red, yellow, and orange burst out –
      an uproar of my intent
      my voice once green turned disparate
         the years of silence fermented

•

A certain silence

a certain softness comes –
        distilled water on dry lips

A certain caution
        floods the warmer parts of your brain
        tumbling down your shoulders
        into your arms –
        and fills the space between them

A silence moves
        down through your chest
                bringing static
                a tingling meant for lovers
                gifting breath

Take these moments
        taste this air, and release them

around you
                A feeling like warm rain
        races to meet you
        desires to cool your worry
and assure you –

        the world speaks
                                of possibility

        •

A word about caution –

being careful works
        in worlds where care was created

But for us – care means

we should never be careful
in a way that spares the architects
                        the inhalers of our recent world

They chose our pain
        based on their own

                        a mirror never holds light for long

•

Somewhere between St. Augustine
    and Nunavut
someone created a policy
    of fear

Somewhere in the hallowed halls
    is a room made for undesirable things
    Behind mahogany doors
        teak tea carts, folded tablecloths
            and discussions on another Indian Summer

the remains
    of our lives lie still

wrapped in the event horizon
    of side glances
        averted gazes
            and cycles not of our making

Nestled deep in these cities
    lie pockets of fear and worry
        cradled in a nest of infinite density ...

        tiptoe past
        breathe lightly
        do not disturb the dividing line
        of undesirable things

        place all your fears
        all your weapons
        place all your waste
        regrets and hesitations

on the other side
    Reserve
    a place for these things
    keep them with us

Maintain a steady stream
    of your fears –
            circling around us

        In time, we will reveal your reflection

•

Sometimes we, too
        wonder where all the abuse comes from

as though we were somehow blinded
by the same ignorance

But we know

        the direction of our madness
        its origin

destruction bleeds
destruction

        •

Bite me

bite the soft flesh

just below my thumb

Watch it bleed
watch my heart roll out over the tabletop
test the creases, and know how my blood
        is anxious to leap out and infect

as you collectively think
so odd, these ones

Suddenly you understand the sharp
        uncontested edges of my thoughts

images shaped like the front end of a burning train
        the black rolling smoke of sighing tires
        the questioning gaze of children

who've witnessed their parents waste themselves

        •

Oh Canada –
how is it that you've come to this?

Where the reverence for life is blackened
and swept under the reverence for systems

and power?

Oh, Canada
where is the humanity that once spoke

of rivers running
the sun rising
partnership

and love?

Oh Canada,
how have you honoured your ancestors?

Would they smile at the numbers
of those you killed?

Do you think
that they would be proud
of the numbers you've lost?

Do you believe
your ancestors
would deny

the life of a child
that was not yours?

Do you feel
this history of disdain
for another is something

your grandfathers would be proud to see?

•

Is there something deeper? we ask
Is there something more?

Is it true that Canada
has settled

and that this is perfection?

                                                                Not to me

for every time someone turns to the wall
when their consumer walks in
when the shame bursts forward in their chest

                                                                Not tonight

for every time someone squeezes their fear
through tiny spaces inside them

                                                                I'll search
                                                                for solitude
                                                                instead

for the shame of repeated harm
upon those who hide their bruises
blood screaming for the body's escape

for every woman, man, and child
pulling their feelings up into the back of their spines
to protect one final piece of themselves

    •

for every woman
whose absence steals warmth

for every child
      killed because we
      are less valuable
      than an ATV

for everyone – for Canada, I say
we are planning our escape

And one day
though you may not understand
we'll insist – finally

not us
not tonight

    •

Do you hear that?

A tiny whisper – asking us to stop

Blood is needed
only when the skin separates
re-knitting
far from the mirrored blades that carved it

and when the skin rejoins itself
after the blood, the flesh

new again

not weaker

but made of things we had

as children

what formed us in the womb

blood is needed only
         when the tear is fresh

when it dries and falls off
it reveals our true strength

•

We need something deeper than flesh
on which to remember ourselves

something greater than a society
which was never ours anyway

    Something stronger than bruises
    and more descriptive of our strengths instead of theirs

something beyond the actions of angry white men
who've long since lost their reverence for life

    Something in the way the world moves
    that Canada forgot

something in the way a Wolf stays silent
careful, observant

not for the aggressor who threatens her young
or herself
but for the impact on her pups

        (trauma is a different death)

    and safe in the knowledge that her family
    stands with her
        a comfort to those
        beside her
        their way of life
        important as life itself

•

Seriously

if wolves are more *civilized* than you

then perhaps you've got it wrong...

•

Once

I think, perhaps, we understood
our humanity got in the way
        of living well

                and we aspired
                to the same harmony
                that animals had

                                        And you fools called it
                                        animal worship
                                                totemism

        •

        .

I was speaking to my mother, inside the house where we built those disgusting memories. My mother was kind, and smiling. She was also holding her head beside her, underneath her right arm. She spoke as if nothing about her recent state could affect the good words she had. And speak well, she did.

After our conversation, she stayed inside while I left the house and travelled to the treeline. Standing there, was a wolf, whom I later would call a friend. She was breathing, slowly – I remember counting in between each inhalation – more than five seconds each. That sound held me with a comfort that never left. I rubbed her back, and noticed a black shape there.

After that, she left. She and others her size ran up and down the inside of the clearing. In their wake, they left something. I looked away, and back again. They were gone. But the hill, the house, and everything in it was covered in snow. I walked into the trees, and turned back one more time. I saw that there was only snow, and nothing remained.

•

It was in a boardroom
that I witnessed the latest killing

A room filled with knowledgeable
white people

trying to understand

what we offer
shaking their heads
not grasping
      the method, our language
      asking – *Would that be recognized by others?*
      (Academics, I presume)

Not seeing the power their world had
over the space

It was in this place that I saw the latest casualty

it was in the silence of the only Indigenous woman in the room
and the anxiety that I could recognize

beaten out of us
by the assertion that we were free to speak
(but not able)

and the ignorance that laid itself that day
in the room, on the table, and covered the room in shame

a shame that white people create
but can't see

I witnessed a murder here this day
when a woman's voice was silenced

with a silent hand that we all recognize
      whether it was in a boardroom
      a jail cell
      a distant farm
      a space between trees and approaching headlights
      or in the face of an officer, standing tall, holding someone's
      jacket and shoes
something they may never see
      and it scares me

•

There's a line
connecting all these things

Its waved form
lends comfort to some

weaves fear for others

precious to some
death for the rest

like diamonds

it's in how we are asked to accept
what is tied into
the skin of this place

where dreams of equity
meet fear and mistrust –
insulated
          by stories of our savage nature

it's how we are crumpled down
by circumstance

rolled tighter
by their refusal to help

as though our health, and happiness
would steal from theirs

and concern for property
overtakes concern
for life

•

We have a word for this
when a person is consumed

by the desire to consume
until a community is devoured –

when fear becomes the person
      and the person
      disappears

when obsession
overtakes the life that birthed it

We have a word
for when strength becomes the person

and the person fades
obliterated by their own creation

Yes, we have a word
for when a person takes

until only they are left
      and they can't separate

      from their desire –

yes, we have a name
      for when something consumes itself
      until nothing is left

Yes
       we have a name for it

but

they called it
a fairy tale

     •

I had a dream that Wiihtikook were chasing us. They were outside the windows of every house, smiling. We could smell their desire – begging for us to show fear, hungry for it.

I knew something would break, either us or them. Before I woke, I saw one standing over us. Their arms were horribly long, and on the ends of them were mirrors, driven, bleeding into their fingers.

I begged myself not to scream.

Screams are their favourite food.

•

How many of us follow
        our dreams?

How many of us wake
        and rethink our day
        according to what we were told at night?

Not many, I suspect

Do we remember the time we turned to the magic that our minds made
        while we slept?

Do we remember

the days when we could share
        the stories our souls wove?

Are there any of us, who would return to a place
        where we didn't seek to control all stories
        where we let our spirit play the strings?

•

Understanding takes special care –
        committing the lines of one's skin
        to memory

repeating flesh
        the sensation of skin on skin

while your mind grasps
a pattern slowly aging

along these lines
revisiting memories seconds old

Changes overcome us
in the short moments
that pass between contact

re-phrasing old thoughts
re-telling old stories
           with new inflections

each movement
a mutation

    •

I dreamed of my sister. It began outside the house built by my mother's abuse. I ran into the house, through the back door.

The light through drawn blinds threatened to breathe me in. I remember running through the kitchen, toward a cellar door that was locked.

Through the back door, burst an angry white bear.

She came in through the kitchen, grabbed my left hand, and bit through the flesh. The blood warmed my wrists, but didn't make it to the floor.

Enough

        I said.

I closed my eyes, and started again. This time, I ran through the back door, locked it, and started toward the cellar door.

The bear came through the door, bit my left hand, and pulled me away – bloody – from the cellar. The blood ran down the sides of her face.

Enough

        I said.

I started again. Through the back door, locked several deadbolts and a chain before I started toward the cellar. Had the locks on the cellar door ready to keep her out.

The bear burst through. I think she had the keys to all my locks. She charged through the kitchen, grabbed my hand, and pulled me toward the exit. Again.

I did not bleed this time. She pulled me from the house, and onto the lawn. I looked at my hand, and wished for blood – blood is how I understood the world.

This time
there was none

-

I dreamed the day my heart broke

My sister wanted me to make a safe choice
        and her gentleness always won

She never demanded anything from me

    •

My sister was witness to everything

Holding her own fear and pain
     she watched with a patience
     only siblings can summon

When we were on the stairwell
     she ran to get help, and disappeared

     I stayed in those chains

     I didn't know how she might appear
     years later

•

After all this
the bruises
    the pain
    the acquiescence
    the misunderstandings

    etching scars in us
    intended to blot our faces out

    we are meant to be ghosts
    among the barely living

    among all this

After all this
memory
    kindness
    healing
    reconnection
    understanding
    the tracing of our lives

    growth beyond lines meant for us

what are we?

    What do we say
    to our children? And to those
    who come after?

•

Tricked
     we forget
     our place

Through loss and terror
     we've stretched the fabric of permanence

     over living things

We've dug up the earth and brought her to stand
     and cast shadows over everything – growing taller
     building in ever smaller spaces

We've preserved
     everything meant to rot and fade
     in boxes, behind glass

TRICKED
We are the mud of a dying swamp
     begging to move

     attempting to turn over the earth
     pulling our muscles and straining
     our faces
     building the cartilage and fluid
     between our harder parts
          straining for our own sense of forever

     moving in a world
     quickly drying
        around us

a world whose lack of elasticity
                    is contagious

So we create
          on the faces of drying stone
          on the dried pulp of our brothers
          in the publishing circles of a world
          designed to hold us in snapshot
          where our histories, our words, our impact
on others
was meant to vanish

          but they forget
          that we are bones –
resurrected from the bones of others
                              Ikonwiwak Kaakiipiniikaaniwaac
Turned to stone
          freed as clay and mud
          supple enough to hold space for other life
          replaced by more life
          proud enough to hold space
          for more bones
          those of our descendants

To the world that we've grown to live in – I say
          remember us well

          •

Remember our resilience

the next time you hear

a crack form
in the foundations
of your concrete shadows

•

We tell stories

That is what we do

Miikwec Nintinaanak Kimishoomisinaanak

Acknowledgments

By some standards, this book of poems took an exceptionally long time to create. As with many beginnings, the threads it has created for me to explore are almost innumerable – and so I write this with great care and concern. I acknowledge everyone who has entered my life. They have all left their mark on these words. I would also like to thank the staff and faculty I met at the University of Toronto's First Nations House and Centre for Indigenous Initiatives: thank you to Alex McKay, Daniel Heath Justice, Deb McGregor, Jennifer Murrin, Eileen and Grafton Antone, Jill Carter, Cynthia Wesley-Esquimaux, Jonathan Hamilton-Diabo, Shannon Simpson, Tracy Jacko, Jackie Esquimaux-Hamelin, Cherie Dimaline, Christine Miskonoodinkwe Smith, and anyone else I've met and failed to mention. This book started while I was a student there, and the community we created made it possible for this work to survive. Thank you for your friendship and advice.

I would also like to acknowledge Lee Maracle for helping me with this work, my writing, and so many other things. You raise me up.

I am incredibly happy that Ovila Mailhot agreed to create the cover image. We are cousins for more reasons than blood; I always felt you understood me – which is, I guess what cousins are meant to do. Love you.

I would also like to thank the faculty and students of the University of Guelph's Creative Writing MFA program. Thank you especially to Catherine Bush, Judith Thomson, Michael Winter, and Dionne Brand. Your advice still runs through my conscience.

Most importantly, I thank my adoptive family, for the journeys we've shared together, and survived together. I love you all.

Nothing would be possible without my sister, my friend, my hero – Kim.

Learning is a lifelong process.

I chose to learn Severin Ojibwe while at the University of Toronto because it was the option that was closest to my original language. I am still learning, and I may one day understand Cree because of it. If you're ever in a position to make the same choice – do it. For the friendships, for personal growth, for increased understanding, for self-love, and most importantly because we don't celebrate effort as much as we could.

Each Ojibwe phrase used in this book infers its own story, telling of a moment I was able to spend with – and learn from – my teacher, my friend.

TYLER PENNOCK was adopted from a Cree
and Métis family around the Lesser Slave Lake area of
Alberta. He is a graduate of Guelph University's Creative
Writing MFA program. He currently lives in Toronto,
where he has worked as an educator and community
worker for over ten years. *Bones* is his first book.